Illinois
The Prairie State

Marcia Amidon Lusted

PowerKiDS
press™

New York

For Patricia Lusted, with love

Published in 2010 by The Rosen Publishing Group, Inc.
29 East 21st Street, New York, NY 10010

First Edition

Editor: Nicole Pristash
Book Design: Greg Tucker
Photo Researcher: Jessica Gerweck

Photo Credits: Cover, pp. 5, 22 (tree), 22 (flag), 22 (bird), 22 (flower) Shutterstock.com; p. 7 © Bettmann/Corbis; pp. 9, 22 (famous people) Getty Images; p. 11 Willard Clay/Getty Images; p. 13 © Kevin Schafer/Getty Images; p. 15 © Al Satterwhite/Transtock/Corbis; p. 17 © Annie Griffiths Belt/Corbis; p. 19 Paul Damien/Getty Images; p. 22 (animal) © www.istockphoto.com/Midwest Wilderness.

Library of Congress Cataloging-in-Publication Data

Lusted, Marcia Amidon.
  Illinois : the Prairie State / Marcia Amidon Lusted. — 1st ed.
      p. cm. — (Our amazing states)
  Includes index.
  ISBN 978-1-4042-8121-9 (library binding) — ISBN 978-1-4358-3368-5 (pbk.) — ISBN 978-1-4358-3369-2 (6-pack)
  1. Illinois—Juvenile literature. I. Title.
  F541.3.L876 2010
  977.3—dc22
                                    2009003300

Manufactured in the United States of America

Contents

Tall Buildings and Open Spaces

There is a state famous for both deep-dish pizza and for being the home of the sixteenth president of the United States. This state has one of the world's tallest buildings and wide open **prairies**. What state has all of these things? Illinois does!

Illinois is in the midwestern part of the United States, south of Wisconsin and west of Indiana. The Mississippi River flows down the western edge of the state. Illinois is called the Prairie State because it once had so much open grassland. It is also called the Land of Lincoln because Abraham Lincoln, the sixteenth president, lived in Springfield. The current U.S. president, Barack Obama, was an Illinois state senator from 1997 to 2004.

Chicago's Sears Tower (center) is the tallest building in North America and the third-tallest building in the world. It is 110 stories high!

Land of the Illiniwek

The first people to live in Illinois were Native Americans. They belonged to a group of **tribes** known as the Illiniwek. The French **explorers** who first came to the area named it Illinois because of this group.

In 1673, the French government controlled the area. They sent Louis Jolliet and Father Jacques Marquette to explore their new **territory**. Many people came from France to settle in the new land. After the French and Indian War, though, France gave up Illinois to the British. After the American Revolution, the British no longer controlled Illinois. Illinois became the twenty-first state in 1818.

This painting shows Louis Jolliet and Jacques Marquette exploring the Mississippi River near Illinois in 1672.

A Part of History

Throughout history, the people of Illinois have played an important part in making jobs safer for American workers. In 1886, some workers in Chicago met in Haymarket Square. They spoke out against their terrible working **conditions**. Police tried to stop them, and many workers were hurt or killed. This is known as the Haymarket Riot. Then, in 1894, workers at Chicago's Pullman Company, which made railroad cars, **protested** against their bad working conditions and low pay.

Working conditions got better. Because of these two events, workers decided to form groups called unions to **protect** their rights. Unions are still around today!

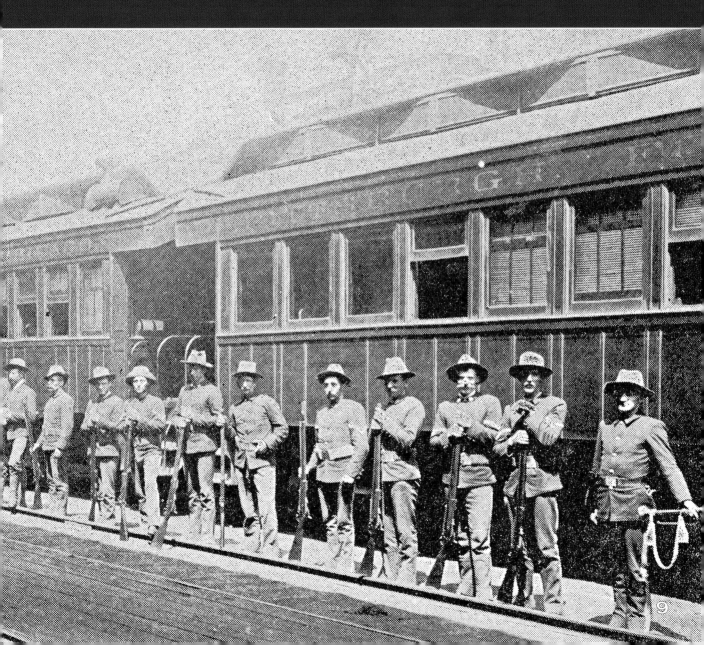

During the Pullman strike, officers had to guard railroad cars from being harmed by protesters.

9

The Prairie State

Much of Illinois was once covered with flat prairies. The rich prairie soil is excellent for farming. In the bottom part of the state are the Shawnee Hills, where cliffs can be found along the Wabash River. Illinois has many other bodies of water, including the Mississippi River and the Ohio River. The northern corner of the state borders Lake Michigan, one of the Great Lakes. The city of Chicago also has its own river, which flows backward, or away from Lake Michigan.

Like most midwestern states, Illinois has hot summers and cold winters. **Tornadoes** are common during the summer months.

This is a soybean farm in Stephenson County, Illinois. In recent years, Illinois has produced more soybeans than any other state.

Bobcats and Bloodroot

Since much of Illinois was covered with prairie, there are not very many large animals native to the state. Raccoons, bobcats, skunks, and river otters are some of the smaller animals that make their homes in Illinois. Hundreds of ducks and geese spend time in the state as well.

Illinois' grassland has many wildflowers, such as the blazing star and bloodroot growing in it. Bloodroot is a white flower that can hurt animals if they eat it. The state flower, the blue violet, grows in woodlands in the early spring. Trees, such as white oak and hickory, can be found in Illinois' forests.

Bobcats are about twice the size of house cats. They generally live in large forests.

Made in Illinois

With so much rich, flat land, Illinois has thousands of farms. These farms grow corn, wheat, and oats. Other farms raise hogs and cows. In the Shawnee Hills, fruit farms grow peaches and apples.

Because it is close to Lake Michigan and the Mississippi River, Illinois has always been an important area for **industry**. Factories there make different types of **chemicals** and supplies that are used for farming and for making food that we eat every day.

Many well-known companies are based in Illinois, too, including John Deere. John Deere is famous for making farming equipment, such as tractors.

This farmer is using a John Deere tractor to move hay. The John Deere Company has been making farm equipment for over 170 years.

See It in Springfield

Right in the center of Illinois is Springfield, the state capital. About 113,000 people live there. People come to Springfield for the Illinois State Fair. Others drive through the city to visit **landmarks** from Route 66, a historic road.

There are other interesting places to visit in Springfield. The Henson Robinson Zoo has **endangered** animals, such as lemurs. If you visit Lincoln's New Salem State Historic Site, you can see what a village from the 1830s was like. You can see a movie outdoors at the Route 66 Twin Drive-In. Most people, however, visit Springfield to see historic places from Abraham Lincoln's life.

At Lincoln's New Salem State Historic Site, shown here, people and buildings are made to look as they did in the 1830s.

Land of Lincoln

Abraham Lincoln is thought to be one of the greatest presidents the United States has ever had. Although he was born in Kentucky, he lived most of his life in Illinois.

Illinois is proud to be the home of the sixteenth president. The people of Illinois are glad to know that such a great man spent so many years in their state.

Many people visit Lincoln's home in Springfield. The Lincoln Home National Historic Site is now a **museum**. Visitors can see what the house was like when Lincoln lived there with his family. They can also learn about his life.

Abraham Lincoln lived in his Springfield home, shown here, from 1844 to 1861.

Enjoying Illinois

Illinois is full of fun things to do. You can visit the city of Chicago and listen to music, play games, and go on rides at Navy Pier. If you are hungry, you can eat a piece of Chicago's famous deep-dish pizza!

If you like sports, you can go to a Chicago White Sox or a Cubs baseball game. You can also just enjoy the beautiful prairies and forests that are found in the state.

Illinois is a great state. Whether you like the city or the country, there is something for everyone to see and enjoy!

Glossary

chemicals (KEH-mih-kulz) Matter that can be mixed with other matter to cause changes.

conditions (kun-DIH-shunz) The ways people or things are or the shape they are in.

endangered (in-DAYN-jerd) In danger of no longer living.

explorers (ek-SPLOR-erz) People who travel and look for new land.

industry (IN-dus-tree) A business in which many people work and make money producing something.

landmarks (LAND-mahrks) Buildings or places that are worthy of notice.

museum (myoo-ZEE-um) A place where art or historical pieces are kept for people to see and to study.

prairies (PRER-eez) Large areas of flat land with grass but few or no trees.

protect (pruh-TEKT) To keep safe.

protested (pruh-TEST-ed) Acted out in disagreement of something.

territory (TER-uh-tor-ee) Land that is controlled by a person or a group of people.

tornadoes (tawr-NAY-dohz) Storms with funnel-shaped clouds that reach the ground.

tribes (TRYBZ) Groups of people who share the same way of living, language, and relatives.

Illinois State Symbols

State Tree
White Oak

State Animal
White-Tailed
Deer

State Flag

State Bird
Cardinal

State Flower
Purple Violet

State Seal

Famous People from Illinois

Black Hawk
(1767–1838)
Born in Saukenuk, IL
Leader of Sauk Tribe

Hillary Clinton
(1947–)
Born in Chicago, IL
Politician

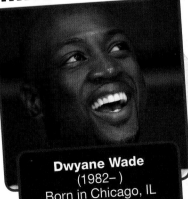
Dwyane Wade
(1982–)
Born in Chicago, IL
Basketball Player

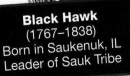

22

Illinois State Map

Legend

○ Major City

✪ Capital

〜 River

Rockford ○
Chicago ○
Aurora ○
Rock Island ○
Peoria ○
Bloomington ○
Springfield ✪

Lake Michigan

Illinois River

Mississippi River

Lake Shelbyville

Carlyle Lake

Rend Lake

Shawnee National Forest

Ohio River

Wabash River

Illinois State Facts

Population: About 12,419,293

Area: 57,918 square miles (150,007 sq km)

Motto: "State Sovereignty, National Union"

Song: "Illinois" music by Archibald Johnston, words by C. H. Chamberlain

Index

Web Sites

Due to the changing nature of Internet links, PowerKids Press has developed an online list of Web sites related to the subject of this book. This site is updated regularly. Please use this link to access the list:
www.powerkidslinks.com/amst/il/